Alienated

This book belongs to

....

Alienated

by Sophie Shortland

THUNDERSTONE
BOOKS

Illustrations and text © Sophie Shortland, 2018.

Edited, designed, typeset, and project managed by Robert and Rachel Noorda at ThunderStone Books.

This book may not be reproduced in whole or in part, in any form or by any means, electronic or mechanical, including photocopying, recording, or by an information storage and retrieval system now known or hereafter invented, without written permission from the publisher.

978-1-63411-007-5 (ISBN 13)

For Tink, my favourite little monster

- Sophie

Aboard the crowded school bus,
I hear the noisy class.
I ignore them and just stare
outside as all the houses pass.

Outside in the playground,
the new girl hides away.
Reluctant to join in the fun,
not wanting to play.

So Mum and Dad invite the new girl,
'round for the day.
They send us both upstairs,
but there is nothing much to say.

We don't need to talk,
and we don't need to play.
Just knowing she is there
makes everything okay.

About the Author

I grew up in Surrey, South East England, with my mother, father, and sister. From an early age, I was obsessed with drawing and creating. Art was always my favourite class and my love for the subject led me to study illustration at Norwich University of the Arts. My goal was to make children's books comparable to the ones that endlessly inspired me when I was a child.

The idea for *Alienated* came from working in a children's after school club. I would observe their behaviour and get them to draw for me at any opportunity. I noticed that a common theme in their drawings was aliens and monsters. Their work inspired mine as I began to develop a narrative around the idea of aliens. I wanted to touch upon a subject matter that hadn't been very prevalent in children's books: autism. I think children's books are a great way to educate and inform children about the world around them. I hope my book educates children about autism or even helps autistic children understand their belonging in this world.

SOPHIE SHORTLAND

Hidden Objects

Yellow Dinosaur

Pirate Bear

Four-Eyed Cat

Fred the Alien

Tennis Racket

CPSIA information can be obtained
at www.ICGtesting.com
Printed in the USA
LVHW07s1526200318
570478LV00014B/31/P